Is This a House for Hermit Crab?

A Richard Jackson Book

Is This a House

by Megan McDonald

Orchard Books • New York

for Hermit Crab?

pictures by

S. D. Schindler

Text copyright © 1990 by Megan McDonald. Illustrations copyright © 1990 by S. D. Schindler.
First Orchard Paperbacks edition 1993

Orchard Books, 95 Madison Avenue, New York, NY 10016

Manufactured in the United States of America. Printed by Barton Press, Inc. Bound by Horowitz/Rae.
The text of this book is set in 18 pt. Novarese Medium. The illustrations are pastel drawings, reproduced in halftone.
Book design by Mina Greenstein.   Hardcover 10 9 8 7 6

Paperback 10 9 8 7 6 5 4 3

Library of Congress Cataloging-in-Publication Data. McDonald, Megan. Is this a house for Hermit Crab? / by Megan McDonald;
illustrated by S. D. Schindler.   p.   cm. "A Richard Jackson book"—Summary: When Hermit Crab outgrows his old house, he
ventures out to find a new one. ISBN 0-531-05855-7 (tr.)   ISBN 0-531-08455-8 (lib. bdg.)   ISBN 0-531-07041-7 (pbk.)
1. Hermit crabs—Juvenile literature. [1. Hermit crabs.] I. Schindler, S. D., ill. II. Title. QL444.M33M34 1990
595.3'844—dc20   89-35653

For Richard

Hermit Crab was forever growing too big for the house on his back.

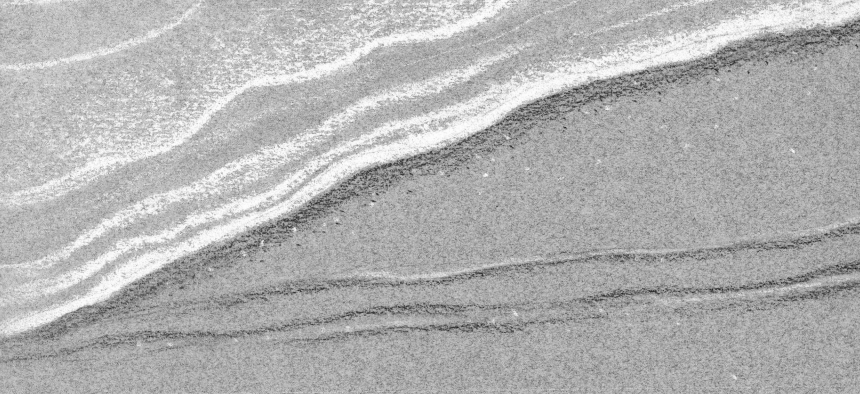

It was time to find a new house. He crawled up out of the water looking for something to hide in, where he would be safe from the pricklepine fish.

He stepped along the shore, by the sea, in the sand . . .

scritch-scratch, scritch-scratch

. . . until he came to a rock.

Is this a house for Hermit Crab?

Turning himself around, Hermit Crab backed his hind legs beneath the rock. The rock would not budge. It was too heavy.

So he stepped along the shore, by the sea, in the sand . . .

scritch-scratch, scritch-scratch

. . . until he came to a rusty old tin can.

Is this a house for Hermit Crab?

When he tried to walk with the can on his back, it bumped and clunked. It was too noisy.

So he stepped along the shore, by the sea, in the sand . . .

scritch-scratch, scritch-scratch

... until he came to a piece of driftwood.
Is this a house for Hermit Crab?
Hermit Crab crawled deep inside the rounded hollow
at one end. It was too dark.

So he stepped along the shore, by the sea, in the
sand ...
scritch-scratch, scritch-scratch

. . . until he came to a small plastic pail.

Is this a house for Hermit Crab?

Climbing up toward the rim, *oops*! he fell right in. He clawed, and he clawed, until he climbed back out. It was too deep.

So he stepped along the shore, by the sea, in the sand . . .

scritch-scratch, scritch-scratch

... until he came to a nice round hole in the sand.

Is this a house for Hermit Crab?

He poked his head down into the opening. A huge pair of eyes blinked back at him. Hermit Crab shivered as he scurried away from the big fiddler crab peering out of its burrow. It was too crowded.

So he stepped along the shore, by the sea, in the sand . . .

scritch-scratch, scritch-scratch

. . . until he came to a fishing net.
   Is this a house for Hermit Crab?
   Poking his claws into the heap, he got tangled and caught. Hermit Crab wriggled and wriggled until he found his way out of the net. It had too many holes.

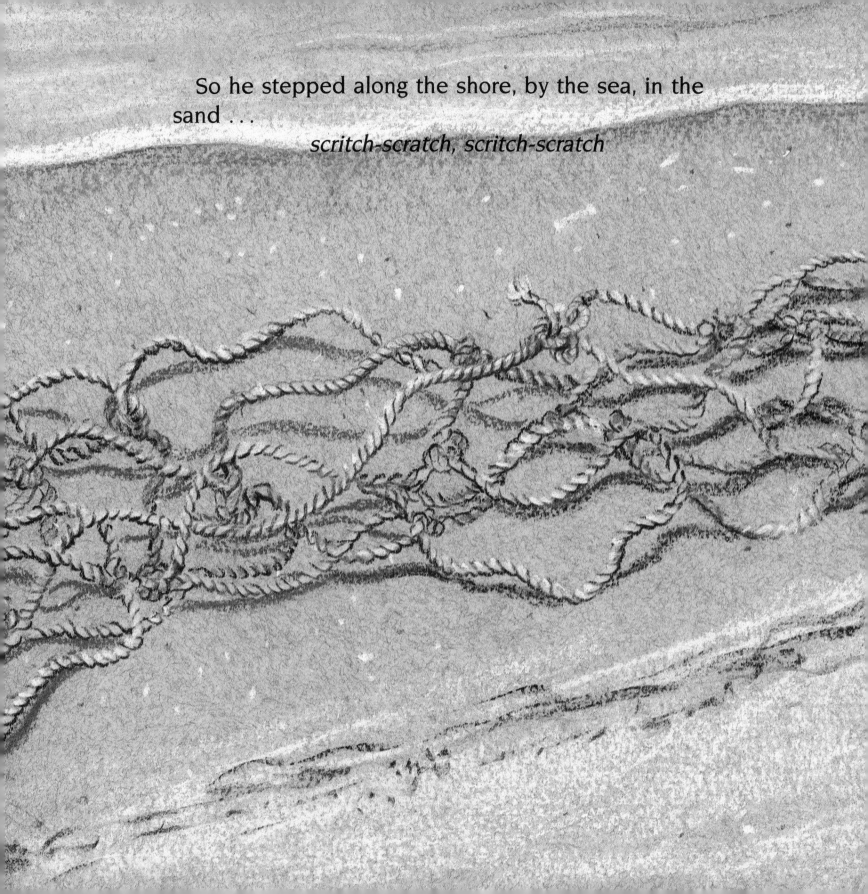

So he stepped along the shore, by the sea, in the sand . . .

scritch-scratch, scritch-scratch

. . . All of a sudden a gigantic wave tossed and tumbled pebbles and sand over Hermit Crab's head. He swirled and whirled with the tide and was washed back out to sea.

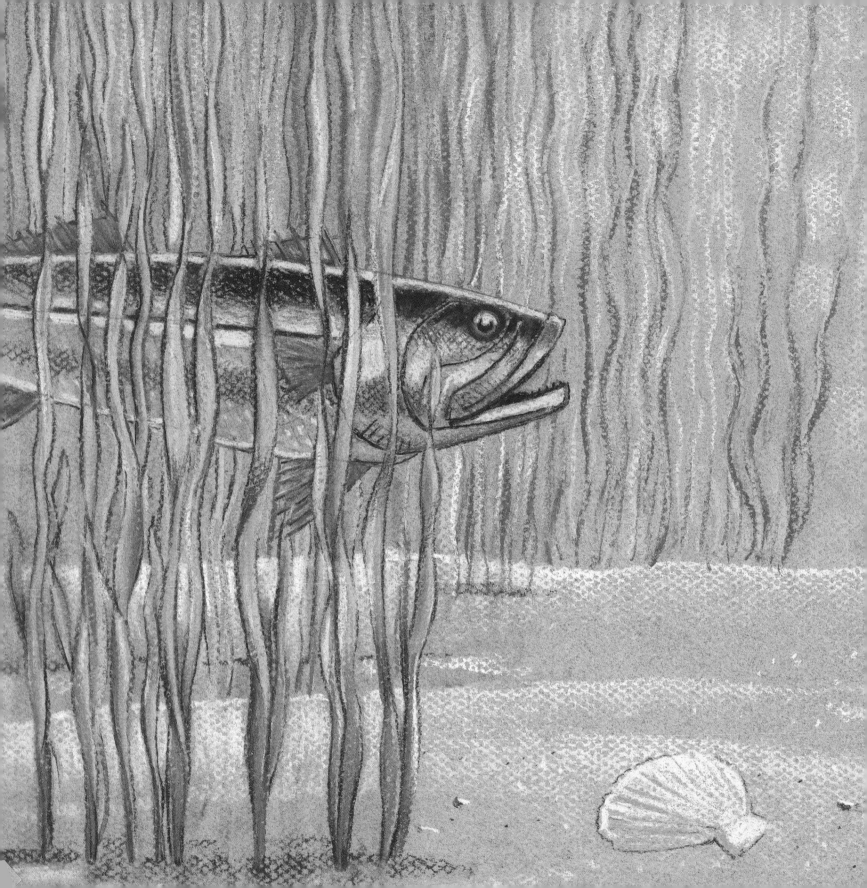

Sleeker than a shark, the pricklepine fish darted out from its hiding place in the tall seaweed. Every spine on its back stood straight as a steeple. Mouth open wide, it headed right for Hermit Crab.

Hermit Crab raced across the ocean floor . . .

scritch-scritch-scritch-scritch

... scurrying behind the first creature he saw.

It was a sea snail, and he hoped it would hide him, but the shell was empty.

The shell was empty!

Hermit Crab scrambled inside as quick as a flash, and clamped his claw over the opening in the shell.

The pricklepine fish circled the snail shell three times, but he could not catch sight of the crab he had been chasing. He glided off in search of something else to eat.

When all seemed still and quiet, Hermit Crab
snuggled comfortably down into his new shell. It was not
too heavy, not too noisy, not too dark, and not too deep.
It was not too crowded and did not have too many holes.

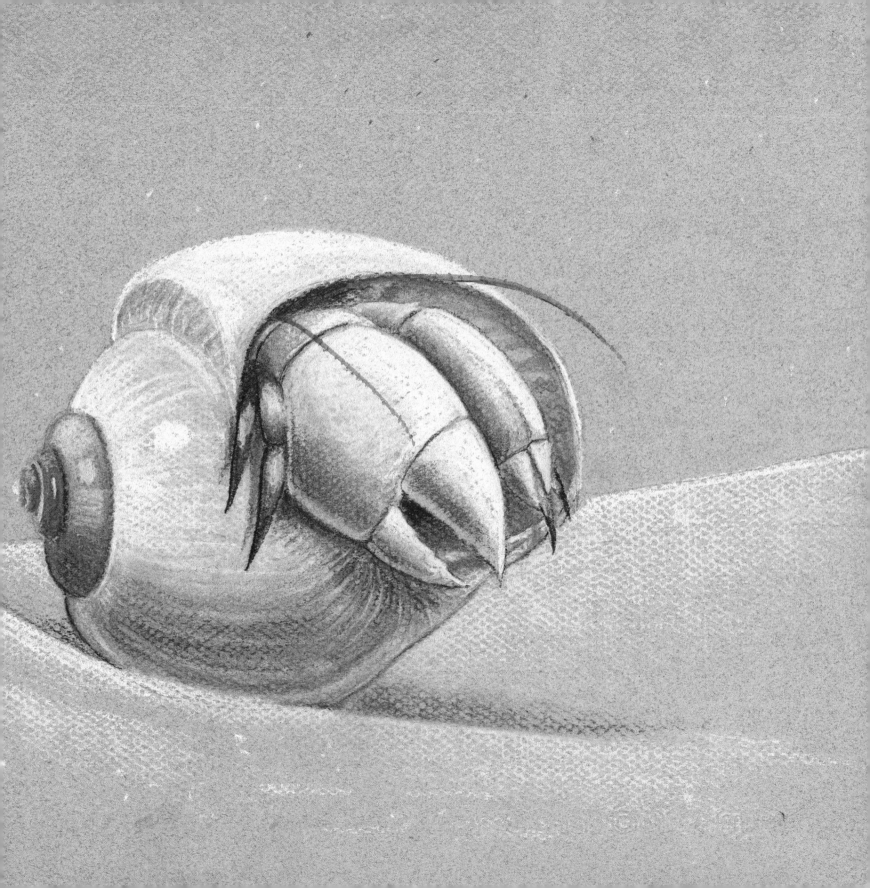

At last, Hermit Crab had found a new home. And it fit just right.